Red Wine

André Dominé

Red Wine

Photography
Armin Faber
Thomas Pothmann

Feierabend

© 2003 Feierabend Verlag OHG
Mommsenstraße 43
D-10629 Berlin

Project Management: Bettina Freeman
Translation from German: Mariana Schroeder
Editing: Lizzie Gilbert
Typesetting: Roman Bold & Black, Cologne
Design: Sonja Loy, Cologne
Lithography: Kölnermedienfabrik, Cologne
Printing and Binding: Christians Druckerei GmbH & Co. KG, Hamburg

Printed in Germany

ISBN 3-936761-53-1
61-04003-1

Contents

USA

Switzerland

Argentina

Chile

to the **World** of **Red Wine**

Austria

Australia

South Africa

world of red wine is colorful.
yet, this is only a small sample
actual variety. Some wines
y make any effort to attract
tion visually. Others appear
st to scream, "Take me!" Some
makers illustrate their love of
n their labels. Others place
trust in the bottle identification
en by their grandfathers. But
seldom that the picture on the
betrays the quality of the
ents. Names of winemakers,
s, landscapes, regions, and
ntries are a far better indication
e enjoyment wine lovers can
ct to find.

Germany

You need to have the right nose. But that's something everyone has. You only need to learn how to hold it in the glass, in order to inhale the intoxicating fragrance according to the rules of the art of wine tasting. Those who want to can then spit it out or stick out their tongues.

This red wine smells of wild berries, black currants, and wild cherries – also of liquorice and vanilla. Another flavor rises to the nose and reminds you of cedar and mint. What great luck if your friends are also "red wine noses."

Famous

They are so numerous that their inclination can be regarded as the norm and hardly merits special attention. They were poets or thinkers, painters or musicians, scientists or statesmen. The philosopher Erasmus von Rotterdam, the author John Gay, the painter Henri de Toulouse-Lautrec, or politicians like Sir Robert Walpole, Napoleon, and George Clemenceau were members of the club. Many contemporary stars of showbiz or politics now even let themselves be photographed with the object of their desire. It apparently inspires confidence to be shown holding a glass of red wine. Many indulge themselves. Napoleon, for example, would never do without his beloved Chambertin Clos du Bèze, no matter where he was. But he also saw to it that none of his soldiers suffered from thirst. Thomas Jefferson, who would later become the third President of the United States of America, must be one of the best-known serious wine lovers ever. During his time as ambassador in Paris between 1785 and 1789, he carefully improved his knowledge of

Red Wine Drinkers

wine. In 1787 he traveled to Bordeaux to gather more information. Afterwards, he dealt only personally with wine merchants and winemakers, thus insuring himself a supply of the superb 1784 vintages from Châteaux Lafitte and Margaux, among others. Afterwards he ordered ample supplies of the not less famous 1787 vintage. Those bottles that weren't destined for the ruling president George Washington, he had marked with his own initials.

In 1985, some of these historic bottles came to light in Paris. On December 5, 1985 Christie's auctioned one bottle of the Lafitte 1787 with the initials Th. J. in London. Publisher Malcolm Forbes bid £105,000 for the bottle, which he bought for his Presidents' Museum. At that time it was the most expensive bottle of wine ever sold at an auction.

Even before coming to Paris, Jefferson had begun cultivating wine grapes on his Virginian estate. For more than 30 years he experimented with vines from Europe, but none of them survived. Finally he had to resort to native American vines.

THE
LOVE
OF
WINE

Red
is the color o'
love. But, as every
one knows, red is also
the color of wine. I'
love is red like wine
can anyone help being a
lover of red wine? Every
man to his taste, and
every woman to hers. Be
it Chianti or Bordeaux
Zinfandel, Lember-
ger, or Mourvèdre –
every wine love.
will surely find
his or he
favor-
ite

"A red wine, please."

Four little words and already you have been unmasked. You are neither a beer buddy nor a boozer. Soft drinks, be they common or exotic, are of just as little interest as mixed drinks, with which the bartender exercises his genius – no matter how spectacular they might be. Nothing but red wine. Nothing else? This order, which appears so simple, inevitably becomes the test by which every pub, bar, restaurant, or hotel is measured. If a glass is pushed before your nose with no further comment, it's best to move along as soon as possible.

But the choice of red wines served by the glass doesn't have to be comprehensive to be convincing. Often a few words suffice to convince you that you're at the right address. Perhaps, "This Montepulciano is the best red we have." Immediately, it is clear you're in the right place and are dealing with someone who understands. How far the common love of red wine will take you, remains to be seen, but you know you have met someone who shares your passion for wine.

2500 B.C.

In Egypt, the first tomb wall-paintings showing wine cultivation and the enjoyment of wine are executed. The vines are trained on trellises. Workers crush the grapes with their feet and ferment the juice in amphorae. In as early as 2000 B.C., wine-makers start recording grape varieties (always red!), the location of the vineyard, and the year of the harvest. Even the owner or manager of the vineyard are sometimes mentioned. Probably these wines have a lot of residual sugar and contain a high percentage of alcohol. In any case, the upper-class society very much enjoys these wines. Some jugs are even left to age.

92 A.D.

Emperor Domitian for-bids the planting of new grapevines on Roman territory and orders vineyards in the provinces – among them Narbonensis, now known as southern France – to be cleared. These measures, which will prove to be un-successful, are aimed at lowering the rising consumption of wine (probably rosé) among his subjects and gaining land for the planting of urgently needed wheat. The law goes into effect but is largely ignored and eventually will be repealed by Emperor Probus in 270.

1150

In the newly constructed wine cellar of the Cistercian monastery Vougeot, the monks succeed in producing a sensation. Instead of filling the barrels imme-diately with must, as has been customary and has produced a pale-colored clairet, they dump the grapes into large fermenting vats and tread them repeatedly with their feet. The result is a carmine colored wine that finally resembles the color of Christ's blood, into which the wine is meant to be liturgically transformed. Dry red wine is born.

1663

In London a wine na "Ho Bryan" causes considerable stir ar connoisseurs. It tas good, has a great c of character, and a deep red color. Arn de Pontac has deve oped this first Bord château wine at his estate Haut-Brion. The vines have the roots in the sandy, pebbly soil known a graves, and the gra are crushed longer than has previously been customary.

Blood-Red Color

2010

After heated debate, the international Wine Parliament has passed a controversial law calling for additives in wine – similar to an existing law governing food products – to be listed on the back label. Among the more than 130 chemical substances that meanwhile can be found in wine, in addition to traditional substances like sulfur and copper, are, for example: phosphoric acid, tetraconazole, azinphosmethyl, fludioxonil, chlorothalonil, oryzalin, dicofol, pyrethrin, metalaxyl, lufenuron, and quizalofopethyl. Wine consumers world-wide have applauded this courageous decision as a long overdue step in the right direction, although it is feared that many medium-sized wine producers will in the future only be able to fill magnum bottles.

1850

Statesman Camillo Cavour, the father of Italian unification, engages oenologist Louis Oudart. He creates the first outstanding wine of the Piedmont using Nebbiolo grapes at Grinzane Cavour. Soon this Barolo will be appreciated everywhere.

1951

Returning from a trip to Bordelais, Max Schubert creates his famous Grange Hermitage out of Shiraz grapes. It is the trail-blazing red wine of Australia.

2000

Not a century vintage, but in many regions a good year for red wines.

Why Red Wine is so Healthy

The news struck like a bomb. In 1991, during the CBS program 60 Minutes, Dr. Se

in France and in Mediterranean countries than in the U.S.A. Further research showed t

small daily quantities, even alcohol with its blood-thinning effects and stimulation of

strengthen the blood vessels, prevent clotting, and protect against free radicals, which

naud explained that, according to a survey, 40 % fewer heart attacks were registered

addition to the Mediterranean diet, regular consumption of red wine is responsible. In

cula- tion can be positive. What's more, red wine contains antioxidant polyphenols. They

>ves the effectiveness of red wine against cancer and Alzheimer's disease.

Bathing

Ever since grape juice has been fermented, people are fascinated by the idea of bathing in wine. They dream of wine as a fountain of youth, from which they can emerge free from wrinkles and full of vitality. Back then they had no way of knowing how close to the truth they had come as they plunged full of hope into tubs of red wine. Phenolic substances, kinds of tanning substances that also prevent clogging of the arteries, are what imparts new firmness and silken shine to the skin. They are found in high con-centration in the seeds of grapes and form the basis of newly developed baths and treatments, called vinotherapy.

in Wine

The best known of the more than 1,000 substances contained in wine (besides water, alcohol, and residual sugar):

Vitamin content (in mg/liter)

	must	wine
ascorbic acid (vitamin C)	38 – 95	0
thiamine (vitamin B1)	0,10 – 0,5	0,04 – 0,05
riboflavin (vitamin B2)	0,003 – 0,08	0,008 – 0,3
pantothenic acid (vitamin B5)	0,5 – 1	0,4 – 1,2
pyridoxine (vitamin B6)	0,3 – 0,5	0,2 – 0,5

Mineral content (in g/l)

	must	wine
potassium	1 – 2,5	0,7 – 1,5
calcium	0,04 – 0,25	0,01 – 0,2
magnesium	0,05 – 0,2	0,05 – 0,2
sodium	0,002 – 0,25	0,002 – 0,25
iron	0,002 – 0,005	0,002 – 0,02
phosphorus	0,08 – 0,5	0,03 – 0,9
manganese	0 – 0,05	0 – 0,05

Polyphenol content (in g/l)

	must	wine
anthocyanin	0,004 – 0,9	0 – 0,5
flavone	traces	0 – 0,05
tannin	0,1 – 1,5	0,1 – 5

The Secret in the Grape

Everything begins with the grape because it contains everything that goes into the making of wine. This cross-section of a red grape shows the pips and the pulp, which makes up 80–90 % of an average grape's weight. The pulp consists of a lot of water and sugar and is light green in color, even in red grapes (except for poor quality varieties.) This poses the interesting question, how can a dark-red wine come from this light-colored substance? The secret lies in the dark-colored skin, which hoards the greatest part of all the substances crucial for the making of wine: first of all those substances producing flavor and color, along with the finest of tannins. Other tannins are found in the pips and stalks. When making red wine, it is important to release these tannins and make careful use of them. The way they are handled is one of the crucial criteria for the quality of the red wine once it is poured into the glass.

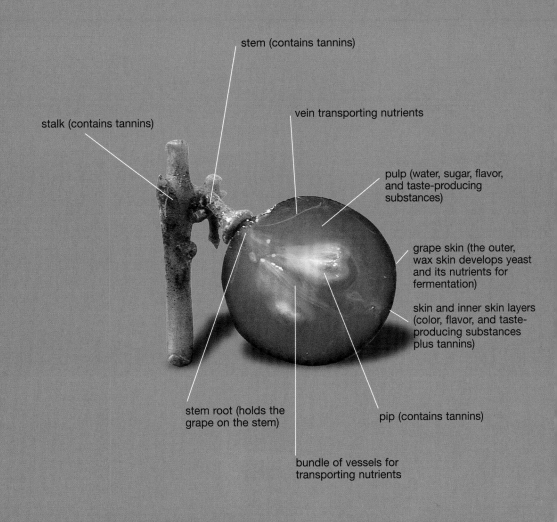

stem (contains tannins)

vein transporting nutrients

stalk (contains tannins)

pulp (water, sugar, flavor, and taste-producing substances)

grape skin (the outer, wax skin develops yeast and its nutrients for fermentation)

skin and inner skin layers (color, flavor, and taste-producing substances plus tannins)

stem root (holds the grape on the stem)

pip (contains tannins)

bundle of vessels for transporting nutrients

1 Merlot
full, round, velvety, fruity
with subtle tannins;
suitable for storage;
world-wide in fashion.

2 Cabernet Sauvignon
very complex, powerful,
notes of cassis and cedar;
tannic; ages well; held in
high esteem everywhere.

3 Syrah
very aromatic, complex, has
a good deal of body, power,
and a touch of tannins. It is
winning ever more fans.

4 Pinot Noir
regarded as the finest type
of grape for red wines.
Superb fruitiness, finesse,
noble tannins; keeps well.

5 Tempranillo
Spain's finest variety,
has a strong fruity note
with elegant tannins;
ages superbly.

**International
Hit Parade
of Red Wines**

TOP

shooting star of the year

6 Sangiovese
number one in Italy in terms of area planted; aromatic, lively tang, fine tannins; can be stored.

7 Garnacha Tinta
or Grenache Noir, has a cherry flavor, volume, is very round; increasingly wines with character.

8 Barbera
from every-day drop to star of the barrel; exciting fruity notes, versatile, has good structure.

9 Zinfandel
California's cult wine; blackberries and fruit; spice and tannins; velvety and full-bodied.

10 Malbec
from Argentina, demonstrates opulent fruitiness and gentle tannins; could become a shooting star.

Nebbiolo

gives the Piedmont unbelievably complex wines that can almost age forever – like Barolo.

Cabernet Franc

recently reaching high form along the Loire; delicious, fruity, velvety body, decisive style.

Mourvèdre

ripening late and exciting with superb tannins; ages very well and reaches great finesse.

Pinotage

South Africa's star variety; intensive red grapes, spicy herb flavor, good structure and potential.

Lemberger

or Blaufränkisch; independent, sweet fruit, good acidity, and fine tannins; suitable for storage.

Secret Tips and Specialties

Cultivation

When thinking of red wine, most consumers think of warm climates. And yet red wines only tolerate warmth in small measures. Most red quality varieties prefer a temperate climate. The best-balanced wines come from areas where the average temperature in summer hovers around 20 °C. When this temperature is clearly exceeded, it is often too much of a good thing. Every winemaker naturally wants to make a good living. But if he wants to produce quality wines, he cannot avoid respecting the soil, carefully preventing disease and parasites, and controlling the yield.

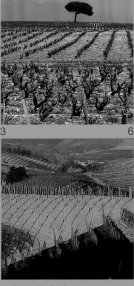

1 Steep slopes along the Ahr   2 An ideal incline in Burgundy   3 Gravelly Rhône-vineyards
4 The terraced Douro Valley   5 Slaty soil in Priorato   6 Limestone marl in Piedmont

The Terroir

What does this often mumbled magic word mean? It means the interplay of soil, alignment, climate, grape variety, and winemaker who is responsible for expressing these elements in his wine. When the terroir is respected, it results in wines with individual, unadulterated, and inimitable personality.

Then wine becomes art. The winemaker is not alone with this task. He needs millions of helpers: Only the intact micro-flora in healthy soil can bring about the exchange between the vine and the earth – or more precisely – the wine and the type of rock. Only in this way does the location imprint its stamp on the wine. That's why the world's best vintners handle their microbes so carefully.

The Harvest

Gathering by hand remains the most gentle way to pick grapes.

It is, without doubt, the highpoint of the year for eve winemaker. He trembles in anticipation as it approache The last two or three weeks before the harvest hav decisive effect on the quality of the wine that ultimate depends on the optimal ripeness of the grapes. Th determines the concentration of fruit sugar in the grape which is responsible for a sufficient alcohol conter The aromatic ripeness is the prerequisite if the arom constituents in the must are to reach their clima Ripeness of the phenolic substances is crucial in re wine and influences the coloring substance (anthocyani and the tannins. Under ideal conditions everything riper simultaneously, but in many years the conscientiou winemaker risks leaving his red wine grapes on the vin a few days longer so that the tannins can ripen, assurir that there will be no undesired "green" taste.

The flowering lays the way for the eventual harvest.

The grapes form quickly and grow for approximately 100 days.

Winemakers check the specific gravity of the must every day.

It's all in the must. The grape skins contain coloring materials, flavor, and tannins. When crushed they come into optimal contact with the fermenting juice. That's what it's about – no more no less.

Must Fermentatio

Pumping out and spraying on top is an effective method of extracting the maximum of color, tannins, and flavor from the solid material.

You can't just leave the fermenting wine alone with the must. After a short time the skins rise to the surface of the fermenting juice. This floating layer, known as the top crust, does not have sufficient contact with the juice. There are various methods to further extract its vital substances. In remontage, the wine is pumped out of the bottom of the tank and sprayed back on top. In délestage, the entire juice is drawn off so that the top crust drops to the bottom of the tank, then the juice is poured back on top of it. The gentlest method is pigeage, in which the top crust is crushed and then pressed down into the fermenting juice, either mechanically or by treading underfoot. These methods assure that the red wine can best absorb its color, flavor, and tannins.

and Pigeage

Barrique

The Celts had one advantage over the
Romans: the barrel. But soon the Romans
were converted and accepted this wooden
"hose" as the perfect wine container, especially when wine had to be transported.
That is why the barrels were constructed
of sturdy staves. The volume varied from
region to region.
Simple wine came in 500–600-liter barrels,
the so-called *Halb-Stück* barrels, which were

so highly prized, a deposit had to be paid
for them. But in regions where better wine
was produced, especially in Bordeaux or
Burgundy, smaller barrels were used.
With the creation of château wines in Bordeaux, barrels increased in importance.
The 225-liter barriques were often renewe
and disinfected with sulfur. Attention was
paid to assure that the barrels were alway
full. For high-quality red wines, storage in

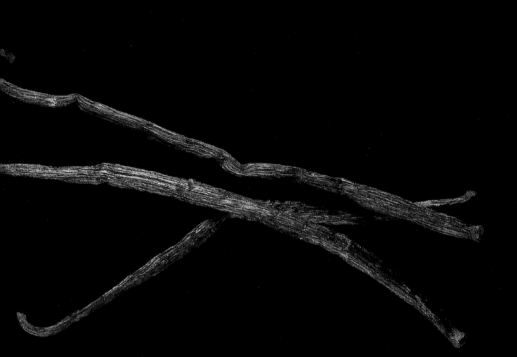

ak barrels is essential. The barrel llows a careful exchange of air. his gentle oxidation helps the vine to ripen, develop its complex avors, and round off the tannins. he barrique mania of our times a new development. With the rogress of modern winemaking, enologists have also discovered he positive effects of new oak

barrels: their vanilla-flavor enriches the bouquet and taste, and their tannins refine the wine. California winemakers were the first to consciously use the best aged wooden barrels. In the meantime, barriques are used world-wide, and wily vintners perfume simple wines with cheap oak chips – a purely cosmetic touch.

Oak chips in the tank imitate barrique aging.

Categories

Lightweights

Reds come in various categories. In the beginning it is best to start with the lightweights. They bring forth a fruity flavor, often possess a pleasant freshness and little tannin. Among them are: Primeur, Beaujolais, Valpolicella.

Middleweights bring the grape varieties and their origin into the ring. It's not the power that counts here, but suppleness and elegance. Pinot Noir and Sangiovese line up in this category, along with many varieties from classic well-tempered wine regions.

of Red Wine

Heavyweights

Attention! Wines in this class have to have vigor and power. Above all they need a firm tannin backbone. You will encounter a good Cabernet Sauvignon, for example from Médoc, also Syrah or Barolo.

In the super heavyweight class are wines with impressive body and a higher alcohol content. Premium Shiraz vies with mighty Napa vattings, Priorato, Châteauneuf, and the best Midi-Crus can easily keep up.

Life Expectancy

1938, 16 years old

Wine has accompanied Styrian winemaker Walter Sk◄ throughout his life. He attributes the fact that today a◄ 80 he still feels sprightly and happy to his daily glass of wine.

But what about the life expectancy of wine? Here the◄ is no room for illusions.

1. No red wine keeps forever. This is especially true of simple table wines or those brought home from vacation.

2. A hard, crude, thin red will never become a noble, balanced wine.

3. High-priced cult wines by no means guarantee longevity. Often their lifespan is unknown.

Note: Every red wine has its individual life expectancy◄ As a rule of thumb, all of them have five phases of development that they must go through.

In their youth they possess the charm of their primary fruit. Ofte◄ this is followed by a rather un-attractive, reticent, interim stage◄ Then the secondary and tertiary flavors begin to unfold until they reach their climax. There they remain for a shorter or longer period before they begin rapidly to fade and lose their flavor. Depending on its structure, each wine reaches these stages at another point in time. A light red keeps one to thre◄ years. Only highly concentrated wines survive for decades.

1942, 20 years old

972, 50 years old

2002, 80 years old

1986, 64 years old

"How long can I store this red wine?" There is rarely a winemaker or wine merchant who doesn't hear this question regularly. And yet, nine out of ten of the buyers who ask this question will have drunk the wine within the next 48 hours!

Shades of Red

Orange
Aged wines with a less stabile color structure shimmer orange, like Barolo and Barbaresco. Orange also appears as a tint on the glass with intensely colored varieties that have reached a considerable age.

Reddish Brown
Many old, concentrated wines have this shade.

Black
Young wines from varieties rich in color like Tannat and Malbec appear almost ink-black when they are produced using extended must fermentation.

Black-violet
Very young, ripe varieties with thick skins, like Cabernet Franc, Syrah, or Zinfandel are this color.

k Cherry Red
nger red wines that are still
h and have high extraction
average color intensity, like
nacha and Cinsault, are this
h dark red.

Light Cherry Red
Wines of low extraction from
the northern cultivation regions
like Germany, or those wines
which are mass-produced,
bear this color.

Dark Ruby
Are wines with a high
color-concentration that
have been in the bottle for
one to two years such as
Bordeaux wines.

Crimson Red
Very young, highly concentrated
wines appear deep red with violet
reflections, for example those made
of Pinot Noir, Nebbiolo, or Barbera.

Medium Ruby
Is the color of wines that are two to
three years old and have an average
structure, like Chianti or Rioja.

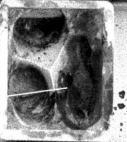

Blue-red
Wines like
Blaufränkisch or
Blauer Portugieser
become this color
when the pigment
is well-extracted.

Violet
Very young wines with
average extraction
from varieties like
Syrah, Dolcetto,
Gamay, or Dornfelder
have a brilliant shim-
mering violet color.

Black Cherry Red
High quality young wines
made of Cabernet, Syrah,
or Tempranillo grapes that
have been fermented a
long time with the skins
are a very deep red with
black reflections.

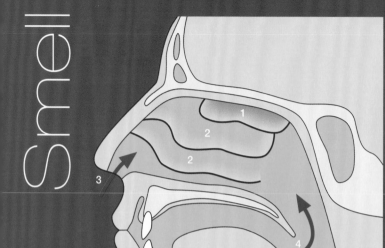

Smell

The smell, "the nose," of a wine is far more complex than its taste. Our olfactory organs are responsible for this. The center, the 2.5-square-centimeter upper meatus (1), is the uppermost of three meati or compartments (2), where ten million nerve cells wait for scent molecules to arrive. These enter the nasal passage when you inhale (3). In the case of experts, this often takes the form of intense sniffing. Scent also originates on the palate (4). The identification of the information given by the olfactory molecules occurs in the brain.

Cross-section of the nasal cavity: The actual olfactory cells (shown here in green) lie under the mucus film between the basal cells and the stroma. They stretch their long thin nerve processes (vacili) from the olfactory bulb to intercept olfactory molecules. Underneath them is the connective tissue.

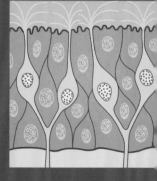

The tongue can only differentiate between sweet, salty, sour, and bitter tastes. The pharynx recognizes texture: thick, thin, or fluid; oily or dry. All flavors also pass through the palate, from which they are transferred to the nasal cavity. That is why experienced tasters often inhale while tasting – so that the air enters the mouth at the same time as the wine. The papillae (see illustration below) in the upper layer of the skin (called epithelium), in which the taste buds are embedded, are especially sensitive near the root of the tongue.

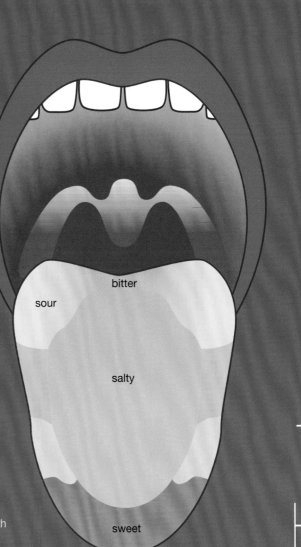

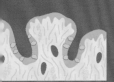

Taste papillae with taste buds.

Taste

Sticking their noses into glasses together is among the greatest pleasure wine freaks enjoy. As much as such events might end in a convivial bout, the relaxed part of the evening has to be delayed. At first concentration is needed both above and behind the glass in order to perceive the sensual impression that every wine arouses. It calls for comparison, analysis, and verbal articulation. First the senses encounter the color of the wine. But it is better to save that for later, when other impressions need confirmation, rather than letting color lead the way.

Tasting and Emptying Reds

f prime importance
the smell of the
ine, its "nose." It
elivers the wine's
ost complex calling
ard. The more splen-
id the wine, the
ultifaceted it is and
e more effort it takes
explore it. Since the

discovery that flavor
is exclusively perceived
in the nose, taste has
lost its former impor-
tance. But it still
deserves your undi-
vided attention. First,
the tongue experi-
ences the basic taste
categories sweet,

sour, and bitter, along
with the texture and
body of the wine. The
palate explores the
wine's diversity, inten-
sity, and length, all of
which bear witness to
its quality. Deeper in
the pharynx, where the
wine slips down the
throat, further exciting
taste experiences take
place – providing it is
a first-class wine. Be
careful not to let the
wine exit too quickly!
It is no accident that
wine, of all foodstuffs,
has the most complex
way of expressing
taste. After lively dis-
cussion of every single
uncorked bottle, little
is left for the happy
group to do, except
the so-called "Belgian
Test," which is to see
which of the wines is
emptied first, meaning
which was the most
popular.

When Many Suddenl

Saw »Red«

Fine red wines, now available in almost every supermarket, were once reserved for a rich and aristocratic minority. In addition, simple, sturdy wines that served the common folk to wash down their meager meals were cultivated in all wine regions. Such wines also were a source of much-needed additional energy in a society where hard physical labor was normal in both rural and urban areas. In the 19th century, a dubious red sea of wine flowed from south to north and served to keep French industrial workers strong and happy. The Gros Rouge (rough red) was born. It would later conquer post-war households in plastic-capped returnable, but none the less star-studded, bottles. The economy slowly improved and the desire for red wine re-awakened even in Europe's gray northern regions. Two-liter bottles of sparkling, sweet Lambrusco, or sweetened Amsel-felder and Kadarkas made the initial contact to red wines easier for consumers. In contrast, the dry, tangy Chianti in its straw fiasco and Valpolicella, which sloshed in with the world-wide pizza fad, almost seemed to be purists. Every Tom, Dick, and Harry went out to eat with the entire family and allowed himself a bottle of wine to go with dinner. Since then, marketing and packaging experts have succeeded in bringing masses of wine to masses of consumers. They don't care if wine comes in plastic bottles or cartons; the main thing for them and their target group is that it is inexpensive.

Red

Spoken

pleasant
gamy
aromatic
blackberry
fine
fleshy
hard
cherry
liquorice
long
longevity
minty
pepper
smoky
rich
round
rustic
velvety
black currant
powerful, robust
tannic
dark
profound
unripe
mellow
complex
big
spicy
cedar

	Français	Italiano	Español
nehm	agréable	gradito, piacevole	agradable
alisch	animal	animalesco	animal
atisch	aromatique	aromatico	aromático
beere	mûre	mora	mora
	fin	fine	fino
chig	charnu	carnoso	carnoso
	dur	duro	duro
che	cérise	ciliegia	cereza
tz	réglisse	liquirizia	regaliz
	long	persistente	largo
ebigkeit	longévité	longevo	potencial de envejecimiento
Minzgeschmack	mentholé	con aroma di menta	mentolado
ikaschote	poivron	peperone	notas de pimiento
hig, geröstet	fumée	con sentore di tostato	ahumado
haltig	riche	ricco	rico
	rond	rotondo	redondo
al	rustique	rustico	rústico
tig	velouté	vellutato	sedoso
warze Johannisbeere	cassis	ribes nero	cassis
strukturiert, kraftvoll	charpenté	ben strutturato, robusto	estructurado
nreich	tannique	tannico	tánico
unkel	foncé	molto scuro	color profundo o oscuro
ründig	profond	profondo	profundo
if	végétal	acerbo	vegetal
chmolzen	fondu	fuso	meloso
ltig	complexe	complesso	complejo
ntig	volumineux	pesante	voluminoso
zig riechend	épicé	con fragranza di spezie	especiado
er	cèdre	cedro	cedra

Drinking

Temperature

is a bad practice world-wide to serve red wine too warm. Even in good

restaurants waiters believe in the room-temperature fairytale. But it has its

origin, like most fairytales, in the time before central heating.

Basically, red wine should never be served warmer than 18 °C – and even

this warm only in exceptional cases. Only very tannic reds need this tem-

perature. Fundamentally there are two things everyone should observe:

The lighter-structured and the fruitier and younger the red wine is, the

cooler its serving temperature should be. The lower limit is around 10 °C. For

example: Primeur and vin ordinaire at 10 – 12 °C; Beaujolais, Valpolicella,

Lemberger at 12 – 13 °C.

The more powerful and older the red wine is, the warmer it should be

served. For example: Chianti, Rioja, Côtes du Rhône, Zinfandel at 14–15 °C;

Burgundy at 15–16 °C; and Bordeaux at 16–17 °C.

Un..

Electric cork lifter

Compressed-air corkscrew

Laguiole waiter's T-form corkscrew with open spiral, foil cutter, and folding bottleneck support

T-form double spiral corkscrew with guide and spring mechanism

Classic T-form corkscrew in modern design

Bell corkscrew made of plastic

Screwpull® with open spiral, guide, folding foil cutter, and removable handle

Double lever corkscrew or butterfly corkscrew with guide

Screwpull® corkscrew with Teflon-coated spiral that is very light and safe to handle

Waiter's corkscrew "Shark" in T-form with folding foil cutter and folding bottleneck support

corking

nly as the last resort should the cork be pushed
to the bottle. Especially since there are unwritten
les that expect outstanding performances during
e procedure…

ince the cork conquered the bottleneck in the
7th century, inventors have been trying to figure out
e easiest way to get rid of it. The most common
oice is the open spiral corkscrew (you can shove
toothpick through the heart of the spiral) with its
arp point that doesn't unnecessarily damage the
ork. Butterfly or waiter's corkscrews use the lever-
ge principle. Other models swivel the spiral into the
ork and force it out effortlessly by way of a second
iral operated by a spring mechanism.

remove or insert cork

Top: A carafe can best be cleaned with warm water and a clean cloth. Oxygen tablets remove sediments.

Above: The "duck" is a classic form of carafe.

DECANTING

Previously, only old wines were poured from the bottle into a carafe. Red wines or vintage ports especially tend to build considerable sediments. To avoid such sediments from landing in the glass and detracting from the enjoyment, you can pour the wine carefully into a carafe, after the bottle has stood upright anywhere from several hours to two days. While decanting, you observe the bottleneck through the light of a lamp or candle so you can stop pouring the moment the sediments come into sight. Small carafes can be advantageous to old wines because they prevent overexposure to the air, and therefore oxidation. The best choice for serving old, valuable vintage wines is the common bottle basket. Many younger wines, on the other hand, need contact to oxygen to bring out the fullness of their flavor. In such cases a large-volume carafe is preferable.

The angle at which the bottle rests in the basket prevents the sediments at the bottom from being disturbed.

G L A

Ripe wines
often have developed
a complex but fragile
bouquet. In order to
enjoy them, you need
a bulbous glass that
narrows at the top.

Young reds
with their intensive fruit
don't need a large bal-
loon glass to be at their
best. A long-stemmed
tulip will better meet
their demands.

Burgundies
like all reds with a
berry flavor are a
best in a rotund
with an only sligh
narrower opening
swings out.

SS E S

Chianti Classico
and other reds with
average body, lightly
accented acidity, and
decent tannins gain
harmony when drunk
from a high glass.

Very strong
tannic reds with a lot of
density need plenty of
air, therefore a large glass
with a high chimney is
the ideal choice.

Velvety
wines unfold and
concentrate their
flavor very well in
wide balloon
glasses that are
only slightly nar-
rower at the rim.

Blind Tasting

"When a wine has more than 95 points, you can't afford it. When it ha
between 90 and 94 points, you can no longer find it anywhere. And whe
it has 89 or less points, no one wants it."

Quotation from an American wine merchant

American Point System

95–100	magnificent, world class
90–94	outstanding
85–89	good to very good
80–84	respectable to good
75–79	average
70–74	below average
60–69	clearly lacking
50–59	fully inadequate

French Point System

18–20	absolute top wine
16–17	outstanding, full of character
14–15	above average to very good
12–13	satisfactory
10–11	not sufficient
7–9	weak with shortcomings
under 7	greatly lacking

German Star System

*****	absolute top wine
****	outstanding, highly recommended
***	good to very good, recommended
**	quite good, satisfactory
*	still acceptable

ren't we all blind when we have wine in the lass whose name, origin, winemaker we now, that we perhaps already drank with oved ones or friends or enjoyed with a suitable lish? Blind tasting grew out of the need to udge quality wine objectively. During such astings it is not the eyes, but the bottles that re covered. The taster doesn't know which intner produced the wine before him. In the ule, wines from one region are tested against ach other, sometimes wines from one grape ariety or market segment are compared. asters concentrate on the smell and taste f each wine and judge its color. Often they nake notes, jotting down key words, then hey award points.

Robert Parker, an American, caused a furor. In his review, "The Wine Advocate," he placed the greatest value on a score of 100 points. Thereby his judgement gained such market relevance that it can, in the meantime, decide the commercial fate of a wine.

The problem with blind tastings is that often 10, 20, and sometimes more wines are tested at one go. Only those that can assert them-selves against the competitors have a chance; wines that are more intense and powerful. Fine, refined wines lose out. It has been proven that this has had a significant effect, especially with red wines, on their style. It is said that some winemakers custom their wines for blind tastings, creating wines that are especially dark, fat, and powerful.

Red Wines

During the last decade classic European red wines have met stiff competition from wines of the New World. Riper, fuller wines with higher alcohol content have met the tastes of consumers. Almost always Cabernet and Merlot are in the foreground. But the future doesn't belong to conformity, rather to specialties. Today, old established regional grape varieties are attracting the attention of vintners and winemakers. At the same time, recently under-estimated regions are proving that they too can produce top-quality products. Good news for all wine fans – the wine planet is rotating again.

of the World

France
Bordeaux
Southwest
Loire

Bordeaux is France's most famous red wine region. Since 1855, its reputation has been carried by the 61 Crus Classés of Médoc. Cabernet Sauvignon sets the tone in the wines of Médoc and Graves and lends them good aging potential and complex character – although they often appear reticent when young. On the right side of the Dordogne, particularly in Saint-Émilion and Pomerol, Merlot reigns supreme. Here the reds charm with their velvety harmony. Other apellations from southwest France have a hard time asserting themselves among the mighty Bordeaux wines. Most successful is Madiran with its contrast-rich Tannat. The most concentrated and long-lived reds of the Loire are made of pure Cabernet Franc.

- ✘ Total vineyards:
  914,000 hectares
- ✘ Wine production:
  5.3 billion liters
- ✘ Bordeaux:
  57 appellations
  110,000 hectares vineyards
  Most important areas:
  Médoc: 69 million liters
  Graves: 20 million liters
  Saint-Émilion: 27 million liters
- ✘ Southwest:
  27 appellations
  Most important red AOCs:
  Bergerac: 38 million liters
  Madiran: 7.1 million liters
  Cahors: 25 million liters
- ✘ Loire Valley:
  42 appellations
  Best red AOCs:
  Saumur-Champigny:
  8.5 million liters
  Chinon: 11 million liters

Right bank of the Dordogne   Super star Pétrus   Château Picon

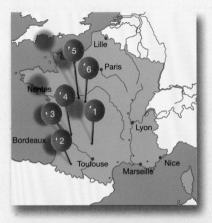

1 Cahors, 2 Madiran, 3 Médoc, 4 Saint-Émilion, 5 Saumur-Champigny, 6 Chinon

Mouton   By the Loire   Saint-Émilion   The Brumonts in Madiran   Chalk cellar in Chinon

Burgundy, Beaujolais, Rhône, Midi

Pinot Noir achieves its optimal expression in Burgundy when it is grown with a respect for nature and with limited yields. Then it produces legendary wines of unequaled finesse. Similarly, Gamay has found its promised land in Beaujolais. It's not the amusing Primeur that shows its true potential, but wines like Morgon, Fleurie, or Moulin-à-Vent. In the northern region of the Rhône valley, Syrah creates unusual wines of unique elegance and harmony. Grenache rules supreme in the southern part of the Rhône valley. The red wines of Provence are Mediterranean in style and harmonious. Winemakers in Languedoc-Roussillon are producing ever more fine, concentrated red wines.

✗ Burgundy:
81 appellations, amo
which 32 are Grands
25,000 hectares vine
Production:
180 million bottles, c
which 75 million reds
Most famous AOCs:
Chambertin, Clos de
Vougeot, Pommard

✗ Beaujolais:
23,000 hectares vine
140 million liters

✗ Rhône:
60,000 hectares vine
290 million liters AOC

✗ Provence:
27,000 hectares vine
133 million liters AOC

✗ Languedoc-Roussillo
300,000 hectares
vineyards
270 million liters AOC

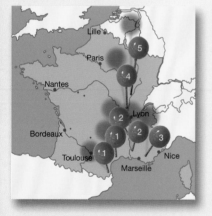

1 Languedoc-Roussillon, 2 Rhône,
3 Provence, 4 Beaujolais, 5 Burgundy

Left: Clos de Vougeot with its Château and winery.

Right: Clos de la Maréchale, Premier Cru of AOC Nuits-Saint-Georges in the municipality of Premeaux.

Left: Grape harvest in front of an imposing manor on the Côte d'Or.

Right: Hospices de Beaune.

Côtes du Rhône from Château Mont-Redon in Châteauneuf-du-Pape.

Left: Roussillon, a village of winemakers, fishers, and artists.

Right: For generations, the vineyards have been passed from father to son, but the fathers never completely step down.

Montalcino in
Tuscany

Enoteca (wine store)
in Verona

In the region of
Chianti Classico

Bartolo Mascarello,
defender of tradi-
tional Barolo wine

Viamaggio in
Tuscany

Italy
Piedmont, Tuscany, South Italy

The demanding Nebbiolo grapes, from which Barolo and Barbaresco – two of the world's greatest and most desired wines – are made, thrive almost only in Piedmont. Tuscany is the home of Chianti and Chianti Classico, as well as Brunello di Montalcino and Vino Nobile di Monte-pulciano, in which Sangiovese grapes with their fruitiness and finesse prove brilliant. But the so-called Super-Tuscans have long since become legendary, too, these are top wines, most of which are based on Cabernet or Merlot. Ever more wines of southern Italy are demanding attention. There, winemakers are astonishing consumers with specialties like Aglianico from Campania or Basilicata; Nero d'Avola from Sicily; or Cannonau from Sardinia.

Barolo is legendary for its aging potential.

- ✗ Total vineyards:
  908,000 hectares
- ✗ Wine production:
  5.2 billion liters
- ✗ Piedmont:
  40,000 hectares vineyards
  350 million liters DOC
- ✗ Tuscany:
  38,000 hectares vineyards
  370 million liters DOC
- ✗ Sicily:
  24,000 hectares vineyards
  85 million liters DOC

1 Sicily, 2 Tuscany, 3 Chianti, 4 Barolo,
5 Piedmont

Ribera del Duero   A great red wine   Sun-soaked Castilians   The Castle of Peñafiel

Spain Rioja, Ribera del Duero, Priorato

Two red wine worlds now come together in Spain. Traditional winemakers bring ready-to-drink wines to market. In the case of Reservas and Gran Reservas they have been aged three to five years or more in barriques or bottles. The modern winemakers follow the international practice, letting their wines age for a shorter period in newer barriques and bringing them to market as soon as they are finished.

Rioja is still the leader with elegant reds in which Tempranillo dominates. A significant portion comes to market as a young fruity wine. Ribera del Duero has established itself as a high-class origin for powerful pure Tempranillo. Priorato, with its grandiose wines from Garnacha and Cariñena, is living proof of the tremendous potential that wines from Spain possess.

- ✗ Spain:
  Total vineyards:
  1,170,000 hectares
  3.2 billion liters
- ✗ La Rioja:
  54,000 hectares
  vineyards
  230 million liters
- ✗ Ribera del Duero:
  12,600 hectares
  vineyards
  24 million liters
- ✗ Priorato:
  1,500 hectares
  vineyards
  1.9 million liters

- ✗ Portugal:
  Total vineyards:
  260,000 hectares
  0.7 billion liters

Portugal

With 500 local grape varieties, Portugal has an enormous potential. In addition, Portuguese winemakers have a keen preference for traditions in the vineyard and in the cellar, without negating the advantages of modern wine technology. In addition to the great red wine regions of Douro, Bairrada, and Dão, Estremadura and Alentejo are attracting ever more attention, thanks to their future-oriented reds.

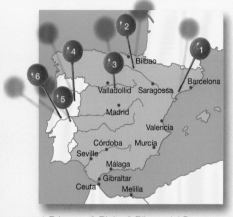

1 Priorato, 2 Rioja, 3 Ribera del Duero, 4 Douro, 5 Dão, 6 Bairrada

The trot of tradition   Time for reds   La Vileilla Baixa in Priorato   Old Garnacha

Germany
Switzerland
Austria

Red wine is booming in Germany where more red is consumed than white. The red cultivation areas are expanding – even along the Mosel. The Ahr region is proud to claim that it is the northernmost red wine area of any merit. But fine Spätburgunder (the German descendant of the Pinot Noir grape) also thrives in Mittelrhein, the Rheingau, and in Baden. There is increasing interest in reds in the Palatinate – also as cuvées. Without doubt, Würtemberg, where superb Lemberger is grown, is Germany's most exciting red wine region.

In the Swiss canton of Ticino, Merlot ripens to noteworthy quality while eastern Switzerland is especially well-suited for cultivation of Pinot Noir. In the canton of Geneva, winemakers have developed a weakness for Gamay. Tastings prove them right. Austria has astonished the wine world with the high quality of its reds. Whether they are made of Cabernet, Merlot, Pinot, Blaufränkisch, or Zweigelt, whether they come from the Weinviertel (Austria's northernmost cultivation region), Vienna, or Burgenland, they offer a great deal of fruitiness and concentration.

✘ Germany: 105,000 hectares, of which 20,000 hectares red varieties
900 million liters
✘ Ahr: 525 hectares, of which 300 hectares Spätburgunder (Pinot Noir)
✘ Switzerland: 15,000 hectares, 120 million liters
✘ Ticino: 961 hectares, of which 93 % Merlot
✘ Austria: 51,000 hectares, 250 million liters
✘ Red wine varieties: 25.5 %
Zweigelt: 9 % = 4,350 hectares
Blaufränkisch: 5.4 % = 2,650 hectares

Wine store
Deutschkreuz

R. Pfaffl Estate
in the Weinviertel

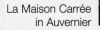

La Maison Carrée
in Auvernier

U.S.A.
California, Washington, Orego

When a Cabernet Sauvignon from Stag's Leap Winery
phalanx of the usual Crus Classés from Médoc far behi
a comparative testing in 1976 in Paris, it was clear to all
lovers that the United States of America could produce su
wines. At first, attention was drawn to the Napa and Sor
Valleys, north of San Francisco. There, in the mean
Rutherford, Oakville, and other towns are now famous for
legendary Cabernets. Further south, Paso Robles
Santa Barbara have made their marks with R
varieties and Pinots. In recent years, wineries in Or
and Washington State have also proven thems
with their high-quality reds. Ever better Pinot Noir
coming from the Willamette Valley in Oregon. Exce
Cabernet and Merlot wines
ripening along the Colu
River in Washington St

- 410,000 hectares vineyards, 2 billion liters
- AVA (American Viticultural Areas):
  85 in California,
  6 in Oregon,
  5 in Washington,
  49 in other areas in the U.S.A.
- Cited grape varieties: at least 75 %,
- Cited AVA: at least 85 %
- Cited vineyards, at least 95 %
- Cited vintage: at least 95 %

1 California, 2 Napa, 3 Sonoma,
4 Oregon, 5 Washington State

Zinfandel   In Washington   Estate in the Napa Valley   Wine auction

Asado near Trivento Popular demijohns Top variety: Malbec

DAMAJUANAS
PARA VINOS

Argentina and Chile

Argentina, in contrast to other South American countries, is a land of wine drinkers. After all, many of its inhabitants originally came from southern Europe. They brought Italian, Spanish, and French grape varieties into the countries, among them Malbec. At the foot of the Andes, Malbec gains wonderful fruitiness and smoothness and produces the most interesting reds in Argentina, followed by Cabernet Sauvignon. The enormous temperature difference between day and night lends them an intensive flavor and elegant structure.

Chile has the most ideal conditions for winegrowing. The nearness of the Pacific moderates the rather dry climate and the many rivers originating in the Andes provide ample water to the vineyards. These conditions allow each winegrower to regulate his yields. Until recently they only produced pure varieties, Cabernet and Merlot. Carmenère is considered to be a specialty, and Syrah is gaining in popularity. Some of the best cuvées prove that not only does Chile produce pleasant wines, but that it also produces great reds.

✗ **Argentina: 213,000 hectares vineyards, 1.6 billion liters**
✗ **Mendoza Province: 144,000 hectares vineyards**
✗ **San Juan Province: 49,000 hectares vineyar**
✗ **La Rioja Province: 7,000 hectares vineyard**

✗ **Chile: 175,000 hectares vineyards (also produce Pisco, grape juice, and table grapes) 0.55 billion liters**
✗ **Maipo Region: 5,100 hectares vineyard**
✗ **Rapel Valley Region: 9,200 hectares vineyard**

1 Rapel Valley, 2 Maipo, 3 Mendoza,
4 San Juan, 5 La Rioja

Traditional pro-
duction in Chile

Always glad to be
on horseback

Red choice at
Concha y Toro

1 Margaret River, 2 Barrosa Valley, 3 Hunter Valley

- ✗ 160,000 hectares vineyards, 1 billion liters
- ✗ Hunter Valley: 2,200 hectares vineyards, 72 wineries
- ✗ Barossa Valley: 6,700 hectares vineyards, 53 wineries
- ✗ Margaret River: 3,000 hectares vineyards, 54 wineries

Australia

Already in the 19th century, winegrowing "Down Under" had reached considerable proportions. At that time dessert wines in the style of Port or Sherry were high on the popularity scale. It wasn't until the 1950s, when many immigrants from Mediterranean countries arrived, that the demand for table wine was established. Penfold's famous winegrower Max Schubert created his Grange Hermitage from the best Shiraz grapes. But it wasn't until 1962 that it became famous and blazed the trail for other winemakers. Australians, who are open to the new advances of technology and oenology, have developed a thoroughly modern wine industry. It reflects the tastes of the consumer and, thanks to experienced marketing techniques, has been successfully exported. Shiraz with its flavor, spice, and rich body has been especially successful, followed by Cabernets and Merlots.

Margaret River

The legendary Grange Hermitage

Tarrawarra in Yarra Valley

At the pioneer Moorilla Estate on Tasmania

Barossa Valley in southern Australia

South Africa

Two events prepared South Africa's winegrowing industry for a new future. In 1991, the abolition of apartheid politics created new interest in South African wines from abroad. And in 1992 the repeal of the quota system, with which the Kooperatieve Wijnbouwers Vereniging (KWV) had controlled the entire production of the country since 1940, infused the industry with new dynamics and led to the foundation of new estates and wine companies. At last, new plantings with healthy imported root stock of world-famous varieties could begin.

Since then South Africa has become increasingly interesting for wine lovers. In addition to inexpensive mass-produced wines, many growers now offer middle to high-quality wines, and they are succeeding ever more often in producing highly attractive wines. The fruity-spicy Pinotage, with its subtle banana flavor, is an exciting native variety. But excellent Cabernets, Merlots, and Bordeaux blends are also grown, for example, in Stellenbosch and Paarl. Walker Bay has proven to be an excellent *terroir* for Pinot Noir.

Tasting at Mont Destin   Franschhoek

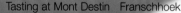

Siesta at Stellenbosch

- 118,000 hectares vineyards,
  660 million liters
- 70 wine cooperatives,
  4,600 wine farmers,
  250 independent bottlers
- Stellenbosch region:
  18,000 hectares vineyards
- Paarl region:
  19,500 hectares vineyards
- Worcester region:
  18,500 hectares vineyards
- Robertson region:
  14,000 hectares vineyards

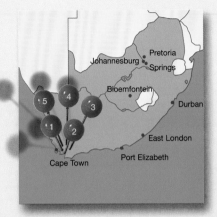

1 Stellenbosch, 2 Walker Bay,
3 Robertson, 4 Worcester, 5 Paarl

pe harvest at Paarl   Vineyard in Somerset   Proud harvest

Wine Festivals

France

✦ Alternating wine villages in Burgundy.
The fourth weekend in January: *St. Vincent Tournante.*

✦ Beaune
The third weekend in November: *Les Trois Glorieuses et Exposition Générale des Grands Vins de Bourgogne.*

✦ Pauillac
The first Saturday in September: *Marathon de Pauillac*

✦ Bordeaux
In July of every even-numbered year: *Fête du Vin*

✦ In Many Beaujolais villages on the third Thursday in November: *Fête du Beaujolais Nouveau*

Italy

✦ Panzano (FI)
The third weekend in September: *Vino al Vino*

✦ Greve in Chianti (FI)
The second weekend in September: *Rassegna del Chianti Classico*

✦ Vagliagli (FI)
The third to fourth weekend in September: *Festa dell 'Uva*

✦ Barolo (CN)
The second weekend in September: *Festa del Vino Barolo*

✦ Dogliani (CN)
One week in September: *Sagra del Dolcetto di Dogliani*

✦ Ora (BZ)
The end of October: *Unterland Wine Tasting Week*

Spain

✦ Tacoronte (Tenerif)
The third week in May: *Semana Vitivinicola alhondiga*

✦ Haro (La Rioja)
In June: *Batalla del Vino*

✦ Valdepeñas
The first week in September: *Fiesta de la Vendemia*

✦ Cariñena (Saragossa)
Middle of September: *Fiesta de la Vendemia*

✦ Logroño (La Rioja)
September 19th: *Fiesta de la Vendemia*

✦ Barbastro (Huesca)
The second half of October: *Fiesta del Vino del Somontano*

Germany

✦ Weinstadt-Beutelsberg
The third weekend in February *Weintreff der Remstalroute*

✦ Stuttgart-Rotenberg
The fourth weekend in May: *Schlossbergfestival*

✦ Mayschoss
The first Sunday in November *Jazz & Wine*

✦ Eltville
The first Sunday in December *Thanksgiving of the Rheingau Vintners*

Austria

✦ Kellergasse Jetzelsdorf
The third weekend in Septemb *Haugsdorfer Hüatagang*

✦ Gumpoldskirchen
The third weekend in September: *Stürmische Begegnungen auf der Sturm- und Mostmeile*

✦ Kellergstetten
The second Saturday in Octob *Poysdorfer Vintners' Race*

✦ Stolzendorfer Kellergasse
The second week in Novembe *Weinherbst*

In traditional winegrowing countries there is an abundance of
wine festivals that are open to
everyone. In any case you have
to pay for whatever you eat or
drink. Sometimes you will only
buy a glass. The number of such
events is so immense, that we
can only list a few to whet your
appetite. In the countries of the
New World, such events are
numerous too, especially in the
United States, in Australia, and
in New Zealand. In the rule they
are organized by individual wineries, usually cater to many paying
guests, and admit only a limited
number of people. In all countries
local tourist bureaus can help
you further. Attention: the dates
listed here can change.

Which Red Suits Her Best?

The relationship between wine and food is often similar to the relation ship between a man and woman. Sometimes one partner dominates, sometimes the other. At times you could eat each other up and at other you can't stand each other. With a bit of consideration it is possible t live together and be rewarded with moments full of passion.

• Fruity reds that are consumed young and drunk cool, are the perfec accompaniment to uncomplicated dishes like pizza and pasta, sausage and ham, casseroles and stews.

• Elegant tannic reds go well with sophisticated partners like carpacc or meat patés, wild mushrooms and wild fowl, coq au vin and beef file

• Full, velvety reds are generous and suit many different kinds of partners. They are especially suited to Mediterranean dishes with lots of vegetables and grilled meats.

• Concentrated, tannic reds are best enjoyed with luxuriant meat dishes with strong sauces. But they can also be enjoyed with roast beef, lamb, or game.

When to Serve Red Wine with Fish

Serving red wine with fish was formerly unthinkable, absolutely monstrous. Today, fortunately, everything that tastes good is allowed and nothing stands in the way of tasteful experimentation. At the same time fish and red wine really are often unsuited to each other. Certainly a tannic monster doesn't go with a fine filet of sole. Concentrated wines and reds with high alcohol content are generally poor choices. But many kinds of fish and seafood, especially if they are fried or grilled, go well with a fruity Beaujolais, Bardolino, or Trollinger, as well as a fine Saumur-Champigny. Grilled salmon, redfish, and tuna go well with powerful reds like Côtes du Rhône or Merlot. Not only does the way of preparing the fish give an indication of which red to serve, but also the ingredients. Turbot served with ceps becomes a gourmet delight when served with an exquisite Burgundy. If monk fish is made with ratatouille, it's perfectly alright to drink a red wine from Provence. When Mediterranean herbs lend a fish their inimitable perfume, then even spirited red southerners make the final cut. And if dried fish is heartily prepared with potatoes, why not serve a Rioja or Navarra for a change?

Drama⬤turgy in Red

Main Course:
Lamb cutlets
with home fried
potatoes and
ratatouille. Served
with a Rioja Gran
Reserva that is at
least six years old.

The starter:
Artichokes *alla
Romana* with
San Daniele
ham. Served
with a pleasant
light Dolcetto.

Dessert: Pears in
red wine (made with
a simple Côtes du
Rhône). As a surprise,
a Californian Zinfandel
with residual sugar is
offered.

The recommend sequence of wines served along with a menu in the past (and occasionally even today) just about amounted to murder. The oldest and finest red wine traditionally arrived with the cheese – possibly an aged, ripe cheese, which with its fat and sharp taste killed the finest red without mercy. It left the wine not the slightest chance of unfolding its filigree and complex, aged flavor. That should always remain foremost in mind when planning a menu. It is possible to begin with younger, lighter wines that can be served at cooler temperatures. And yet, if you want to open an old red, this may be the best moment, because the wines that follow it should be more concentrated and tannic. Hearty, well spiced but not overly salted dishes go well with them. The crowning glory of the meal may then be accompanied by a velvety, noticeably fruitier, yes even a semi-sweet red wine.

Cheese: Ami du Chambertin, Soumatrain, Cîteaux, or Chèvre from Burgundy. Served with a still young Pinot Noir from the Côtes de Nuits in Burgundy.

So It Ages

Put to bed in the light of day like our Bacchus-like Adonis, the wine is sure to develop wrinkles, because light is one of the worst enemies of aging wine. Close behind are warmth and swings in temperature. A temperature above 15 °C will noticeable speed up the ripening process in the bottle. Continual ups and downs in temperature don't allow reds to come to rest and can also lead to corks springing leaks. High humidity is positive, shaking or odors are not. Red wines bedded in humid cool cellars can age for decades, provided they have the necessary structure.

The best vintages

are always those that you have on hand. You just have to know how to handle them. Anyone who really takes vintages into serious consideration when buying wine should study a number of important wine regions. Bordeaux alone is not enough. Wine freaks have a standing rule: "In poor years buy wines from great wine-makers and in great vintage years buy from small winemakers." Weak vintages can provide a great deal of pleasure when drunk young. Average vintages need a few more years to ripen, but only great wines from great vintages should be aged for decades or set aside for your heirs.

Left page: This is the way Austrian wine-Adonis Leo Hillinger goes to bed.

A well-stocked cellar is an exciting view for wine lovers.

Red Wine and

What's the point of speaking soberly
about this relationship – and pointing
out that red wine improves circulation
to the brain, supplies it with oxygen,
thereby increasing the ability to feel all
types of excitement and consequently
arousing the libido? Who doesn't
know that red wine helps us forget
small barriers that formerly separated
us from our good fortune? Isn't it
much better to say that red wine
comes in the color of love, saturated
with warmth that only awaits the
opportunity to be shared and makes
the skin of your partner so smooth…

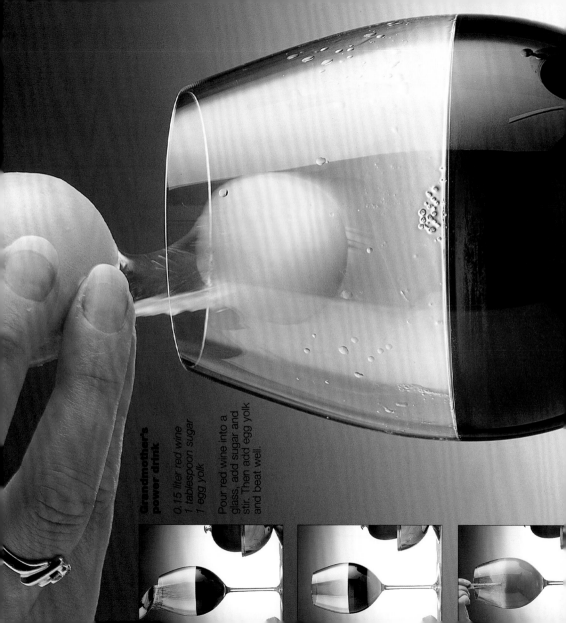

Grandmother's power drink

0.15 liter red wine
1 tablespoon sugar
1 egg yolk

Pour red wine into a glass, add sugar and stir. Then add egg yolk and beat well.

Drinks with Red Wine

Turkish Blood

1 unsprayed lemon
ice cubes
1 bottle red wine
1 bottle sparkling wine

Slice lemon into thin strips, remove pips and place into a two-liter carafe. Add ice cubes and pour red wine over them. Let steep for twenty minutes. Remove the lemon slices and add chilled sparkling wine.

Claret Cup

3 tablespoons sugar
0.1 liter Port
20 ml Curaçao
juice of 1 lemon
1 bottle Bordeaux
1 bottle mineral water
10 strawberries
1 strip of cucumber peel
a pinch of nutmeg

Mix sugar with Port, Curaçao, and lemon juice in a pitcher. Add Bordeaux and mineral water, stir well. Add strawberries, garnish with cucumber peel, and grate nutmeg on top. Serve cool.

Manhattan Cooler

4 glasses red wine
20 ml Rum
2 tablespoons sugar
juice of 2 lemons
mineral water
ice cubes

Place all the ingredients except water and ice in a mixer jar and mix well. Put ice cubes into four long-drink glasses. Pour mixture over the ice and add mineral water to fill the glasses.

Beurre rouge
Red Wine Butter
(for 6–8 portions)

100 g. shallots
250 g. butter
0.25 liters Côtes du Rhône
1 tablespoon chopped parsley
salt, freshly ground pepper

Finely chop the shallots and cook in 1 tablespoon of butter. Deglaze with red wine, reduce, and cool. Beat the rest of the butter until foamy and fold into the reduced mixture. Season with salt and pepper. This is especially good with steaks.

Boeuf Bourguignon
Burgundy Beef
(for 4 persons)

1 kilo beef shoulder
100 g. smoked bacon
200 g. onions
300 g. carrots
50 g. butter
salt, freshly ground pepper
2 tablespoons flour
3 cloves of garlic
1 bouquet garni
1 bottle red Burgundy

Cut the meat into rough cubes, dice the bacon and vegetables. Melt butter in a Dutch oven, brown the meat first and then the vegetables. Season with salt and pepper and sprinkle flour on top. Add garlic, bouquet garni, and red wine and braise for two hours.

The RED in the Kitchen

Neither corky red wine, nor one turning to vinegar, nor the leftovers of an overly oaky fashion wine belong in the kitchen. There, simple honest wines that have not been oak barrel-aged are the best, for example, Pinot Noir and Merlot, Sangiovese and Garnacha, Côtes du Rhône, reds from the Midi and southern Italy. Avoid wines that are very tannic or have high acidity. Reds are indispensable when it comes to marinating and braising red meat or game. And Coq au Vin, a chicken cooked in Pinot Noir, is delicious.

Oh Gosh! A **Stain!**

The greatest passion for red wine experiences a crises when a full glass is poured over the table, tablecloth, skirts or trousers, shirts, sweaters, and jackets and flows all the way to the carpet. *Quel malheur!* It is best to react quickly. A good old household trick is to generously sprinkle salt on red wine stains on clothing and tablecloths. Leave the salt on the stains for five minutes, then rinse well. In carpets it is sufficient to brush out the salt. Commercially produced stain removers are helpful when the stain has set. If you don't have one at hand, dissolve two tablespoons detergent in a glass of warm water and apply to the stain. Rinse with clear water and pat dry. By the way, if you want to discover the most fantastic way to remove red wine stains…

...we recommend you consult our book on **White Wine.**

Red Websites

U.S.A.
www.demystifying-wine.com
www.winepros.org
www.wineinstitute.org
www.oregonpinotnoir.com
www.washingtonwine.org

Australia
www.wineaustralia.com.au
www.winepros.com
www.winetitles.com

South Africa
www.wosa.co.za
www.wine.co.za

France
www.vins-bordeaux.fr
www.vins-medoc.com
www.chateau-latour.fr
www.chateau.figeac.com
www.interloire.com
www.chateau-de-villeneuve.com
www.bivb.com
www.domaine-rousseau.com
www.beaujolais.com
www.vins-rhone.com
www.chateauneuf.com
www.languedoc-wines.com

Italy
www.agriline.it
www.astidocg.it
www.brunogiacosa.it
www.chiantinet.it

www.avignonesi.it
www.sassicaia.com
www.fonterutoli.com
www.masi.it

Spain
www.riojawine.com
www.riojaalta.com
www.do-ribera-duero.es
www.principedeviana.com
www.enate.es
www.torres.es
www.enovins.com (Balearic Islands)

Germany
www.deutscheweine.de
www.vinum.com
www.winepage.de
www.cogsci.ed.ac.uk/~peru/
German_wine.html
www.germanwine.de

Austria
www.weinausoesterreich.at
www.austrian.wine.co.at

Switzerland
www.wein.ch
www.winecity.ch

Argentina
www.argentinewines.com
www.wineplanet.com

Chile
www.winesofchile.com

Photo Credits